the great physician

Lilian B. Yeomans, M.D.

Gospel Publishing House/Springfield, Mo. 65802

02-0729

Contents

THE GREAT PHYSICIAN
(Formerly published as *Divine Healing Diamonds*)
Copyright 1933, 1961
by the
Gospel Publishing House
Springfield, Missouri 65802
Printed in the United States of America

ISBN 0-88243-729-1

Foreword

That the ministry of healing played a very important part in the growth of the Early Church is abundantly evidenced by the New Testament, especially the Book of Acts, and the first centuries of church history.

On their way to the temple to pray, Peter and John were appealed to by a lame man, crippled from birth, and therefore a perfectly hopeless case. Undaunted by his condition, they obeyed literally the instructions given them in Mark 16:18 and laid their hands on him in the name of the living Christ, who was working with them. As a result, the man leaped up, stood, and walked, and leaping and praising God, followed them into the temple.

"And all the people saw him. . . ." (Acts 3:9). "And all the people ran together unto them" (Acts 3:11).

"And though persecution arose, many believed, and the number of the men were about five thousand" (Acts 4:4).

The heart cry of people today is still, "Sir, we would *see Jesus*" (John 12:21). Jesus saving, Jesus healing, Jesus baptizing, Jesus coming in the clouds in great glory. When they *see Him* they will run toward Him.

That this little book may be used to help them to see Him as the "Healer of every sickness," the Great Physician, is the earnest prayer of the writer.

LILIAN B. YEOMANS, M.D.

1

Thirty-five Years of Divine Health

At the conclusion of a Bible reading I gave some time ago, a number of people crowded around me to ask for prayer, counsel, and so forth, and I dealt with them, according to their various needs, as the Lord enabled.

All the time that I was doing this I was aware of the presence of a silver-haired lady, a stranger, who was gazing intently at me from the very edge of the group. She made no move to approach until the others had dispersed. Then she came up to me and, looking right into my eyes, said, "Can you tell me where I can see Dr. Lilian B. Yeomans?"

I said, "*Look* at me."

Her eyes seemed to try to pierce my very soul as she further inquired, "Are you that dope woman that I saw one day, years ago, clinging to any support within your reach to keep you from falling, and in spite of it you did fall on the floor from very weakness?"

"Yes; I am that woman," I replied.

And when I had convinced her of my identity she related to me the story of meeting me in the most deplorable condition while I was still "hurt with fetters" and "laid in iron" before the King sent and loosed me on that glorious and never-to-be-forgotten day, the 12th of January, 1898.

The dear woman's incredulity made me realize as never before how marvelous was the miracle God wrought in me when, all those years ago, He delivered me from the last stages of narcotic addiction, into which I had fallen through overwork in the practice of medicine and surgery.

It was almost impossible for her to credit the evidence of her senses when she saw "that dope woman," after thirty-five years, not only rejoicing in health, strength, vigor, and tireless energy, but actually engaged in confidently pointing others to the source of these, the river of the water of life, clear as crystal, proceeding out of the throne of God and of the Lamb, for "everything shall live whither the river cometh."

Yet such has been my occupation for thirty-five years, and, praise God, such is my delightful task today!

Thirty-five years of divine health, life more abundant, superabounding vitality! For though I was strong and robust before my constitution was wrecked, and my whole system poisoned by the large quantities of lethal drugs, sulphate of morphine, and chloral hydrate (my steady diet, though I toyed with a number of others), which I took daily in the dark period of my abject slavery to narcotics, I can truly say that there is a sense in which I never knew, before I accepted Christ as my physical life, what it means to *Live*.

Let me try to tell some of the things it means to me. First, victorious life for the body. Not that I have always been exempt from Satan's attacks on my physical being, but, through the continuous inflow of a river of life from the indwelling Christ, these have been repelled.

Second, the promises of God turned into facts in bones, muscles, nerves, organs, and tissues.

Third, it means, at times, the most delightful buoyancy and all-around sense of physical well-being imaginable, far exceeding the "joy of life" which used to make me want to hop, skip, and jump incessantly as a child.

Fourth, it means that when I am not mounting up on wings like an eagle, or running without resultant weariness, I can walk and not faint. "Jog trot, jog trot, jog trot" — that is the pace that kills by its ceaseless continuance and awful monotony. It brings me to the very end of myself, but "we which live are always delivered unto death for Jesus' sake, that the life also of Jesus might be made manifest in our mortal flesh" (2 Corinthians 4:11).

> And now the flesh must daily die
> Beneath the chastening rod,
> Yet see the inner man renewed
> By hidden Bread from God.
>
> O bruised Meal that wasteth not;
> O Oil that cannot fail!
> And thus I see that mighty Hand
> Here in my flesh prevail.

I find my strength assured by boarding at Elijah's boardinghouse, the home of the widow of Zarephath. "The barrel of meal shall not waste, neither shall the cruse of oil fail," for they symbolize the "life also of Jesus" manifest in our bodies. When you come to the end of your strength you find Omnipotence.

These thirty-five years have not been spent wrapped up in cotton wool or reclining on flowery beds of ease. God forbid! I shall praise Him throughout eternity for the privileges He has accorded me in traveling thousands of miles, on the King's business, addressing thousands in His name, and praying for thousands of unsaved, sick, and burdened ones. Also for the exalted privilege of feeding His sheep.

And all of this is a tiny fragment of what thirty-five years of divine health have meant to a one-time "dope woman"!

This story "will be continued" in eternity.

2

"A Woman of Canaan"

"Jesus . . . departed into the coasts of Tyre and Sidon. And, behold, a woman of Canaan came out of the same coasts, and cried unto him, saying, Have mercy on me, O Lord, thou son of David; my daughter is grievously vexed with a devil. But he answered her not a word. And his disciples came and besought him, saying, Send her away; for she crieth after us. But he answered and said, I am not sent but unto the lost sheep of the house of Israel. Then came she and worshipped him, saying, Lord, help me. But he answered and said, It is not meet to take the children's bread, and to cast it to dogs. And she said, Truth, Lord: yet the dogs eat of the crumbs which fall from their masters' table. Then Jesus answered and said unto her, O woman, great is thy faith: be it unto thee even as thou wilt. And her daughter was made whole from that very hour" (Matthew 15:21-28).

Do you not love to plunge your hands into the Bible, that casket of rarest gems, and bring them up dripping with sapphires of eternal truth, emeralds of undying hope, and flashing faith diamonds? God's

throne rests on a pavement of sapphire — "a rainbow
. . . like unto an emerald" encircles it.

Out of what darkness these diamonds are mined
oftentimes. Here is one, a Kohi-noor, Great Mogul,
and Eastern Star, all in one; blazing, flashing, gleaming, glittering, glowing, sparkling, scintillating, a star
of the first magnitude in the gospel firmament, a
"treasure of darkness," mined out of the broken heart
of a "woman of Canaan."

"A woman of Canaan!" An alien from the com-
monwealth of Israel, a stranger from the covenants of
promise, without Christ, having no hope, and without
God in the world.

"A woman of Canaan!" A devotee of the most
ferocious and licentious forms of heathenism that ever
blotted the pages of history with crime and tears and
blood.

"A woman of Canaan!" Yet destined to wear forever on her bosom, placed there by the Son of God
Himself, an order of merit beside which all earthly
decorations and distinctions are but tinsel, and the
very stars of heaven fade into dimness! "O woman,
great is thy faith!"

Everything was against her. There was absolutely
nothing in her favor. Very possibly she had never met
a follower of the Lord Jesus Christ or heard a Scripture passage read. But somehow a word of God had
been borne to her by the "wind (that) bloweth where
it listeth."

Maybe a neighbor said, as he returned from a trip
to Galilee, "I saw the Man of Galilee yesterday."

"You saw Him? What was He doing?"

"Healing sick children. A mother laid a little, pale,
puny baby in His arms and He just patted it gently

and looked up and the baby laughed and crowed with glee, and began to play with Him. He surely loves children."

"Did He say anything?"

"Yes; He stretched out His arms and said, 'Come unto me all ye that labor and are heavy laden, and I will give you rest.'"

"Are you sure that He said that? just that exactly?"

"Just that."

"He didn't say, 'Come unto me all *Jews* that labor and are heavy laden'?"

"No; He said 'all.' But where are you going?"

"To Him. He said for me to come, didn't He? If anybody is heavy laden I am sure I am with that poor, tortured, writhing girl of mine."

But when she comes to Jesus she is met with — silence! How can He refuse to answer her when He bade her come? When the disciples beg Him to get rid of her — they are ashamed to be in her company — He answers in a way that seems to close the door of hope to her forever: "I am not sent but unto the lost sheep of the house of Israel." He was only teaching the baby to walk by faith.

But when she presses to His very feet He uses language so apparently harsh that one would think she would flee, affrighted and affronted — "It is not meet to take the children's bread, and to cast it to dogs." He called her "a dog," a type to the Oriental mind of everything unclean and loathsome, to bring her to a realizing sense of her exceeding sinfulness.

Her path was beset with difficulties, but difficulties are the food on which real faith thrives best. It must be tried as gold is tried in the fire. The Lord Jesus saw in her true metal that would stand the fire and come out gleaming brighter than ever. So He plunged her into the furnace, because He loved her and longed to see her shine as the stars, forever and ever.

The way up is down, and before honor is humility. Jesus brought her to a sense of sin, and when she had taken her place as a poor, wretched sinner, a vile dog, He was able to exalt her to the place of highest privilege, and put the key of His treasure-house into her hands.

Nobly she met the test. See the faith-gold gleam in her simple answer! "Truth, Lord" . . . Thy Word is truth. And may we not imagine her saying to her own heart, "I take the place it assigns to me. Yet I will not despair. A dog, but even a dog has provision made for him." And then to the Master: "Thou wilt not deny to me the dog's portion, the crumb that falls from the Master's table. It is all I crave. Thou canst not deny it!"

And He could not. He places in her outstretched hand an unlimited order on His unsearchable riches.

"Be it unto thee even as thou wilt," and with it bestows an encomium worth more than all the plaudits ever received by earth's greatest ones: "O woman, great is thy faith: be it unto thee even as thou wilt. And her daughter was made whole from that very hour."

3

The Man with the Withered Hand

It is only by faith that we can please God and fulfill His will. To believe on Jesus Christ is *the* work of God, that is, the work that He requires of us, from which all lesser works necessarily flow (John 6:28, 29). They, the lesser works, are inevitable, however, for "Faith without works is dead" (James 2:20).

> You can't get to heaven in a rocking chair,
> The Lord won't have no lazy folks there.

This is the work of God that you believe, and it is *work* and not play.

If ever a man was certain of numerous progeny, Isaac — to whom offspring as the dust of the earth and the stars of heaven had been promised, and upon whose betrothed wife, Rebecca, the blessing "Be thou the mother of thousands of millions" had been invoked — was that man. Yet it was not till the Lord was "intreated of him" for his wife, who was barren for twenty years, that Esau and Jacob made their appearance upon the stage of human history. Isaac had to take the blessing by faith.

Yes, to "turn promises into facts," as Dr. Northcote Deck puts it, you have got to work the work of God; walk the walk of faith, and it takes two feet to walk it, to "pray and take." You may hop around forever on one foot, praying, praying, praying, and get nowhere. If that is your case put down your "take" foot this moment and march on to victory. Even Isaac had to do it; it is the only way through.

In Luke 6:6-11 we find a flashing faith diamond, a "gem of purest ray serene," a man who "took," though his right hand was withered and he had nothing to take with. Jesus was teaching in a synagogue and saw him with his withered hand, powerless, no grasp to appropriate, no grip to retain, no punch to fight.

Dr. A. B. Simpson commented on this passage: "So many Christians have no hands! They have no grip in their fingers, no stamina in their will, no hold in their faith." If that be so with any of us, let us not forget that there is healing for spiritual, as well as physical, paralysis with the Great Physician.

To return to the scene in the synagogue, we note that there was a powerful opposition present. There always is; look out for it! That is always the case when God manifests His power.

The scribes and Pharisees were doing the work of their master, the accuser of the brethren, and though they were silent, Jesus knew their thoughts.

He knows yours and mine too. It is not enough to keep our faces smug and our tones honied. Let us pray, "Let *the meditation of my heart* as well as the words of my mouth, be acceptable in thy sight, O Lord, my strength and my Redeemer!"

The Lord Jesus began dealing with this man by commanding him to do what he could: "Rise up, and stand forth in the midst." In other words, He made him take higher ground and publicly confess his abject helplessness and utter dependence upon divine power for deliverance.

People would rather conceal their deficiencies if possible. A German emperor who had an atrophied arm exhausted the ingenuity of artists, who painted and photographed him, in their efforts to provide poses that would hide the deformity.

This man, however, met the test. Faith always does what *it can*. But it never stops there. It wouldn't be faith if it did. It goes further and does what *it can't do*. Faith is the work of God, and He demands the impossible. "Ye must be born again." You can't do it, but you must do it. No choice about it.

"Be ye holy . . ." You can't do it, but you must do it. No choice about it. "Be ye clean. . . ." (As disease pollutes every drop of blood it is essentially unclean, and this Scripture involves a command to be whole, as well as holy.) You can't do it, but you must. No choice about it.

To return to the man with the withered hand, Jesus has told him to do what he can do and he has obeyed. Now comes the command to perform the impossible.

"Stretch forth thy hand!"

"And he did so: and his hand was restored whole as the other."

How did he do it? The only way it can be done. He worked the work of God, believed on Him whom God hath sent (John 6:29); knew that Jesus never fails; that His commands are enablings.

With God all things are possible, and all things are possible to him that believeth, for faith makes room for God to work and thus releases omnipotence.

Sometimes the simplest things serve to make the sublimest ones clear to our understandings. Nothing has ever helped me to realize just what faith is so well as my youthful experience in learning how to mount a horse when I was only a chunky child, with little length of limb, and no spring in me.

My father was a surgeon in the U.S. Army, and we were stationed at a frontier post in northwestern Texas, where an officer kindly undertook to teach me to ride.

I was wild with delight and perfectly fearless, so I was soon prancing around like a regular cavalryman. When my teacher arrived he always found me mounted and ready for my lesson. There was a reason for this which he never suspected. The only way I could mount the animal — a huge mettlesome charger belonging to my father, which seemed to me as high as a battleship — was to lead him round to the chicken coop and roll off the roof onto his back.

One day my teacher was expressing his satisfaction with my progress in equestrianship to another officer, when the latter replied, "Oh, she rides well enough when once she is mounted, but it's a scream to see her mount. Did you teach her to roll off the roof onto the horse's back?"

The next time my teacher came I met him, ready mounted as usual, when to my horror, he said with the voice he used when he was drilling the troops, "Dismount."

"Oh, please don't make me dismount. I don't want to."

With a dangerous glint in his eye he said once more, "Dismount," as though I was a regiment of cavalry, and I was on the ground in a moment. Then he said, "Now you will mount properly."

"No, thank you. I don't want to go riding today."

"You will go riding today, after you have mounted properly."

He held out his hand and made me touch it with the tips of my toes — of course it was all side saddles and long shirts in those days — and then said, "Spring." And I *couldn't, but I did.* And the next thing I knew I lighted in the saddle as easily as a bird flies. For I only tried to spring and my instructor's strong right arm did all the rest.

That is the way you can "take" that precious thing for which you are longing and praying. Take it *now.*

Then stand upon His Word, which endures for aye,
For God will bring it to pass;
The elements will melt in your sight some day,
But His Word will God bring to pass.

Yes, God will bring it to pass,
Yes, God will bring it to pass;
It does not depend on you, or it never would come true,
But God will bring it to pass.

4

The Man Borne of Four

"It came to pass on a certain day, as he was teaching, that there were Pharisees and doctors of the law sitting by, which were come out of every town of Galilee, and Judæa, and Jerusalem: and the power of the Lord was present to heal them. And, behold, men brought in a bed a man which was taken with a palsy: and they sought means to bring him in, and to lay him before him. And when they could not find by what way they might bring him in because of the multitude, they went upon the housetop, and let him down through the tiling with his couch into the midst before Jesus. And when he saw their faith, he said unto him, Man, thy sins are forgiven thee. And the scribes and the Pharisees began to reason, saying, Who is this which speaketh blasphemies? Who can forgive sins, but God alone? But when Jesus perceived their thoughts, he answering said unto them, What reason ye in your hearts? Whether is easier, to say, Thy sins be forgiven thee; or to say, Rise up and walk? But that ye may know that the Son of man hath power upon earth to forgive sins (he said unto the sick of

the palsy), I say unto thee, Arise, and take up thy
couch, and go into thine house. And immediately he
rose up before them, and took up that whereon he lay,
and departed to his own house, glorifying God. And
they were all amazed, and they glorified God, and
were filled with fear, saying, We have seen strange
things today" (Luke 5:17-26).

There is a beauty about a cluster of gems that
oftentimes surpasses even the exquisite loveliness of a
solitaire. I was looking at some single stones the other
day, blue, yellow, green, and pure white ones; then I
gazed at some clusters and they seemed fairly ablaze
with every conceivable color of flame. Here in this
scripture passage we have a splendid cluster, a magnificent group of five great blazing gems. Faith diamonds!

Please note the setting carefully. You have noticed
that diamonds are often placed on black onyx to en-
hance their brilliance. Or they are worn over black
velvet. So this cluster of faith diamonds is surrounded
by the blackest, most determined, most persistent unbelief recorded in the New Testament.

It was not a matter of individual unbelief, but of
corporate, national unbelief. For this occurrence took
place at a regular convention, a concerted gathering,
at which were assembled Pharisees — the acknowl-
edged spiritual leaders of the Jews, respected, nay
revered, by all the people — and doctors of the law,
learned men versed in the Scriptures and esteemed
as authorities in all matters relating thereto. These
were assembled from every town "of Galilee, and
Judæa, and Jerusalem."

There can be no shadow of doubt that they had
come for the express purpose of investigating the

claims of Jesus as the expected One; the Messiah who was promised to Israel. To investigate, nay to carp and criticize; to criticize God incarnate, Immanuel, God with us! And yet the sacred record adds, "And the power of the Lord was present to *heal them.*"

> Grace, Grace, marvelous Grace,
>   Grace that will pardon and cleanse within,
> Grace, Grace, infinite Grace!
>   Grace that is greater than all my sin!

And it was not God's fault if any of them went away unhealed.

There is never a person who comes to a healing meeting, I care not how sinful or how sick he may be, but that the power of the Lord is present to heal him. God is not willing that any should perish. He wants to save and heal all. Even if they are carping and criticizing He desires to bring them to repentance and faith and to heal them. It is said of our Lord Jesus Christ that He went about doing good and "healing *all* that were oppressed of the devil, for God was with Him" (Acts 10:38).

Now these magnates filled the house where Jesus was teaching so that there was no room for real seekers. There they sat occupying every inch of space, listening with ears that were deaf to the divine power of the message; gazing with eyes blinded lest the light of the glorious gospel should shine into them; refusing to enter themselves and preventing others from entering. There are people today who are regarded as spiritual leaders who are doing that very thing.

Into this darkness enters the cluster of flashing faith diamonds. The man borne of four.

How do we know that the paralytic exercised faith?

Because he allowed the four bearers to carry him, help-less, palsied creature that he was, into a struggling mass of humanity. I spent years in hospitals and I can assure you that it took faith on his part. Many and many a time I have known paralytics refuse ab-solutely to permit themselves to be moved. If it were done, in spite of their protestations, they would rend the air with their cries and groans.

It is hazardous enough to go into a mob like that if you are possessed of all your physical powers, but to allow yourself to be thrust into it when you are a perfectly inert mass of impotence takes faith.

Try as they might the courageous four could not find by what way they might bring him in because of the multitude.

Did they give up? Did he cry and whimper, "Boys you shouldn't have brought me. Take me home. I only hope I may live to get there." No: he had *faith*. Faith doesn't know how to give up. Do you remember when Elijah was praying on the top of Mount Carmel and sent his servant to look towards the sea to see if there was any sign of the rain for which he was pray-ing?

The servant came back and said, "There is noth-ing." And Elijah said, "Go again." And he returned with the same message and received the same instruc-tion. And again, and again, and again it was repeated. There could be no giving up. *God had promised.*

So, to return to the paralyzed man and his four bearers, may we not imagine this conversation?

"We are going to hoist you up the side of the house, and let you down through the roof."

And his replying, "I don't care what you do with

me as long as you lay me at the feet of Jesus. That's the place for me."

He must have been not only willing but anxious, or they would never have attempted such a difficult and dangerous procedure. I have directed the transfer of too many helpless patients not to know that.

Nothing would stop them, the fearless five; faith knows no fear. They tear up the roof; doubtless the owner of the house expostulates, and we may imagine the conversation continuing:

"Never mind, Neuben; we will make you a new roof that will beat this all to pieces, when he is healed."

"I'll mend it with my own hands," adds the paralytic.

"Easy there, boys," as they begin to lower him.

"All right, down you go; you'll walk home," from the faithful four.

And, with indignant gaze the dignified rabbis behold this ignorant man, unversed in the Law of Moses, actually about to tumble on their reverend heads. To avert this catastrophe they hastily take them out of the way. And the paralytic reposes restfully at the feet of his Redeemer.

Those who have reached that haven of rest after battling midst the fierce waves of physical anguish and mental torture know what blessed quietness fills the entire being there. To alter the dear old hymn a little:

> From every stormy wind that blows,
>   From every swelling tide of woes,
> There is a safe, a sure retreat,
>   'Tis found at Jesus' sacred feet.

5

At the Beautiful Gate

Apparently the friends of this unfortunate man had done all in their power to aid him. Day after day they washed him, dressed him, fed him, and carried him to the Beautiful Gate of the temple where his pitiful plight was sure to appeal to the sympathies of worshipers in that sacred place. And they had persevered in this benevolent work for years, for we are told that the man was "about forty years old" at the time of his healing. But let us note that all that human effort could accomplish left him *outside* of everything worth while.

It was a beautiful gate but he was on the wrong side of it. A gate is something through which to pass to something beyond: an entrance, a portal, to the supply of your needs, the satisfaction of your longings and desires, the fulfillment of your aspirations.

How perfectly the condition of this sufferer typifies the state of unregenerate humanity!

By nature we are outside the Beautiful Gate, "far off," without God and without hope; "strangers from the covenants of promise."

It doesn't matter how people may cleanse us by

reform methods, or how resolutely we may endeavor to cleanse ourselves; how we may be dressed up in culture, morality, and refinement, we are still outside the Beautiful Gate.

We may be borne along on our own native resolution, or the will power of others, to the very portal; but we cannot enter; for Jesus has said, "No man cometh unto the Father, but my me." *It takes Jesus to bring you in.* And how ready He is to do it! See where He comes, in the persons of two of His representatives, Peter and John, and of them the lame man "asked an alms."

What a poor, imperfect prayer! But a prayer nevertheless, and oh, the power of prayer! He *asked,* and One has said, "Ask, and it shall be given you; seek, and ye shall find; knock, and it shall be opened unto you; . . . everyone that asketh receiveth." Everyone that asketh, no matter how imperfectly, receiveth.

Many years ago I heard a woman address an audience of thousands in one of the great cities of the world. She has been in the Homeland for a long time now, and it is not necessary to mention the name by which she was known on this earth. Suffice it to say that she bore a title of nobility and had been closely associated with royalty. She was educated, cultivated, accomplished, graceful, and beautiful. She lived in a splendidly appointed house and had been brought up in a most dignified church where she was accustomed to sit in cathedrals, with the light pouring from windows of amethyst, ruby, and topaz stained glass, and to listen to the sobbing of great organs and the oratory of famous ecclesiastics, and murmur responses out of a prayer book to the prayers prescribed by the ritual.

She didn't realize that she was outside the Beautiful Gate till one day when stark, staring, shameful tragedy stalked into her home, and she had to find a living Christ to help her bear her unsupportable burden. Under the shadows of the trees of her ancestral woods, at evening, when the dusk was falling and the stars were beginning to shine, she cried: "Oh, God, let me know that You are!" for truly she was outside everything. Quick as a flash came the answer. "Act as though I was and thou shalt know that I am."

So real was the message that she replied, "I'll do it." Into the house she went to pick up her Bible; to fall upon her knees; and in a few moments she found herself inside the Beautiful Gate, brought nigh by the blood of Christ. How astonished people were! I could not begin to tell you how wines were banished from her home, how prayer meetings took the place of balls and dinner parties, how she forgot to send cards to the dukes and duchesses and instead invited the poor and lowly. Yes, prayer, even a poor imperfect prayer, if heartfelt, will work wonders.

Now to return to the lame man who is still outside the Beautiful Gate. In answer to his prayer Peter says, "Look on me." It matters everything where you look. The power of a look! It brings what you look for right into your soul and body. It changes you into what you look at.

"We, . . . beholding as in a glass the glory of the Lord, are changed into the same image." Beholding . . . the glory of the Lord we *are changed into the same image*. God says so. There is life, spiritual life, physical life — for a look at the Crucified One.

And the lame man obeyed; gave heed to them,

expecting to receive something of them. Looking and expecting, he could not be disappointed. Neither can you. Look *and expect,* this moment. Those who do this are never disappointed.

But right here Peter carefully explains to the man just what he may expect from *Peter and John,* and that is exactly and precisely nothing. No more and no less.

"Silver and gold have I none."

"We're bankrupt, so far as I go. Personally I couldn't heal you of a wart on your finger, or the smallest corn on your little toe." That is what Peter would tell us if he were here this moment, and by actions if not words he said further: "Nevertheless look on us and see through us, and in us, Another, who is Almighty; whose will it is to heal all who call upon Him! 'Such as I have give I thee.' "

"Then you have something?"

"Yes," he could have answered, "I have the Name, which conveys the power of Jesus the Son of God. Utterly bankrupt and perfectly helpless in ourselves, we are nevertheless the accredited agents of Omnipotence. *'In the name of Jesus Christ of Nazareth rise up and walk.'* "

And the lame man, looking steadfastly with the eye of faith, saw no longer feeble human beings but ambassadors for God, plenipotentiaries, through whom God is operating. He yields to the kind, warm grasp and lets himself be lifted up. And immediately — the response to immediate faith is instantaneous — his feet and ankle bones receive strength, "and he leaping up (Oh, the bouyancy, the ecstasy of newborn faith!), stood, and walked, and *entered with them into the temple.*"

Blessed moment of fruition! He passed through the Beautiful Gate, at which he had gazed longingly for so many weary years, and entered "with them" . . . the apostles of the Lamb, with the redeemed of all ages, into the temple, the house of God! There he is, where no human hand could ever have led him, where no self effort could have placed him, and he is quite at home, for he leaps, and walks, and praises God.

This is the first recorded miracle of healing in the Holy Ghost dispensation. As that is the era in which we are living, we have a right to expect that God will work, in answer to implicit faith, just as mightily today. And we shall not be disappointed if we cast ourselves upon Him and trust Him wholly.

Are you outside the Beautiful Gate? Don't stay there. Yield to the kind, strong arm that is held out to lift you up. It is the arm of Omnipotence, though it looks no larger than a man's hand. The Beautiful Gate will swing open for you and you will enter into the fullness of the blessing of the gospel of Christ.

6

A Covenant and the Contradiction

God made a covenant with Abraham. He said to him, "My covenant is with thee, and thou shalt be a father of many nations. Neither shall thy name any more be called Abram, but thy name shall be Abraham" (father of many nations); "for a father of many nations have I made thee" (Genesis 17:4, 5).

Abraham had a covenant with God, who is ever mindful of His covenant, who remembereth it forever, who confirmed it with an oath, swearing by Himself, because he could swear by no greater. Abraham also had, in his bodily condition as revealed by the evidence of his senses, an absolute contradiction to the provisions of the covenant God had made with him.

God's Word pronounced Abraham fruitful, with progeny as the stars of heaven, and as the sand upon the seashore for multitude. Common sense pronounced him, so far as possible paternity was concerned, as dead as the rods of the rebellious princes of the children of Israel when Aaron's rod budded, and produced blossoms, and yielded almonds, before their startled gaze.

The whole world sided, and sides, with the common sense view, that is, judging after the sight of the eyes and the hearing of the ears. Let us not forget that, while we are in the world, we are not of the world.

Let us not, after singing lustily, "Do not look for me way down in Egypt's sand, For I have pitched my tent far up in Canaan's land," be found walking in the "counsel of the ungodly" (Psalm 1:1), who refuse to believe the promises of God and . . . to call "those things which be not as though they were" (Romans 4: 17).

Athanasius, the intrepid champion of the true deity of our Lord Jesus Christ against the attacks of the Unitarians, Arius, at the Council of Nicaea, A.D. 325, was warned by a wishy-washy well wisher, "Have a care, Athanasius; the *world* is against you."

"Then I am against the world," he replied.

Athanasius against the world! Believers are necessarily "against the world." They cannot for one moment accept worldly beliefs and standards, for "All that is in the world . . . is not of the Father" (1 John 2:16). Thank God, like Abraham and Athanasius, they are also overcomers of the world, for "This is the victory that overcometh the world, even our faith" (1 John 5:4).

But, to resume the thread of our meditation, Abraham, the covenant, and the contradiction. How did he reconcile these two irreconcilables? You remember what they were: God's Word which declared him the father of nations, and the deduction of human reason, based upon the evident physical impossibility of his begetting offspring.

Now get your mouth ready for a delicious morsel,

a luscious tidbit, a spiritual feast. Abraham *didn't reconcile the two.* He didn't even attempt to reconcile them. There could be no necessity for such reconciliation for, as Abraham well knew — "What *God's Word says is . . . is.*"

Having *divine light* upon conditions, why give a moment's thought to deceptive appearances? Under such circumstances they are to be *ignored utterly.* This is the only course a believer can consistently, and safely, pursue, for "Whatsoever is not of faith is sin" (Romans 14:23).

"Considered *not* his own body, now dead . . . and it was imputed to him for righteousness. . . . It was not written for his sake alone . . . but for *us* also."

Yes; God has given us a covenant, *"I am the Lord that healeth thee"* (Exodus 15:26). Claim it; meet the annexed conditions by the power of the indwelling Christ. If you fail, fly like a bird to your Mountain:

> "Death and despair, like the sea waves cold,
>   Threaten the soul with infinite loss;
> Grace that is greater; yes, grace untold
>   Points to the Refuge, the mighty cross."

Then, stand fast in the liberty, physical as well as spiritual, wherewith Christ hath made you free.

When Satan comes along with some bodily appearance, or sensation that contradicts the covenant God has made with you covering healing and immunity from disease, what are you to do? "Consider not your body." Consider the covenant. Consider the Apostle and High Priest of our profession whose precious blood seals the everlasting covenant.

"Consider not." Blessed words! Unfailing refuge from all the fiery darts of the wicked one; "Consider not." Heavenly atmosphere in which no disease germ can survive for the fraction of a second! Consider not." Do not accord to physical symptoms a passing thought: ignore them. Refuse to take them into your calculations. Would that I had some medium, other than cold ink and dry paper, in which to convey to you the blessedness of the relief from distressing symptoms of all kinds that *invariably* attends this Abrahamic method of meeting contradictions. Invariably? Yes; I repeat it, *"invariably."* "Jesus *never* fails." "According to your faith *be it unto you"* stands, though heaven and earth pass away.

"O why don't these distressing symptoms disappear? I was prayed for by the elders according to James 5:14!" Your speech betrayeth you. You are considering your own body and that is why they persist.

"But," some one asks, "Is it possible to 'consider not your own body' when it so unpleasantly, even painfully, obtrudes itself upon your notice?"

Yes; it is *gloriously* possible, for the God of Abraham is our God. As we unflinchingly take our stand on the naked promise, there springs up within us the "faith of God" (Mark 11:22, margin) which makes walking on the water a delight, and swinging out over the aching void with nothing beneath us but His Word, heavenly bliss. Hallelujah!!!

7

A Bible Birthday Party

Everybody has a birthday and most of us have sometimes enjoyed celebrating it by giving a party and feasting our friends at a table adorned with a beautiful birthday cake, all ablaze with lighted candles, receiving appropriate gifts, and in various other pleasant ways.

That being the case, I think we cannot fail to be interested in studying a Bible birthday party, especially that of such a mighty man of God as Caleb, the Son of Jephunneh, the Kenezite, of the tribe of praise (Judah).

Oh, how they would make the very heavens ring with the praises of God, and the atmosphere vibrate with His power, for we read that God inhabiteth the praises of Israel. There is no party in all the world that is so ecstatically blissful as one where everyone belongs to the tribe of Judah (Praise). I remember such a gathering at which a very solemn Scotchman was present. At least, he was very solemn when he came in and I feared that he did not belong to the tribe of Judah. But if not, he changed his tribal allegiance for, as we were lifted into the very presence of God on great waves of adoration and wings of praise, his face shone, and he murmured to me, "It's heavenly revelry."

I believe that was what Caleb's birthday party was like. I don't know if he had a birthday cake, but if so they had to put 85 candles on it. But was he downhearted? No, No, No! Was he wrapped up in cotton and hot-water bottles? By no means. He was interested in one thing only and that was his *birthday present*.

It was this way: forty-five years before God had promised it to him, and after waiting all that time without a doubt or a fear he boldly comes to claim it on his eighty-fifth birthday.

Isn't it a wonder that he didn't get discouraged and give up and die long before that? Oh, no; that was the farthest from his thoughts. He couldn't think about dying, hadn't time to die in fact, for there was that promise to be claimed and proved up on first.

The very thought of that birthday present had kept him alive. Now you are all aquiver with curiosity to know what this wonderful present was. If you will read Joshua 14:6-15 you will learn that the birthday present was a mountain full of giants, the Anakims (Numbers 13:33). It was his tonic, his stimulant.

The thought of that mountain had kept him alive. But what about the giants on it which he had to over-come before he could take possession? Why, he tells us in Numbers 14:9 that they were his "bread." He fed on them in thought continually, and waxed stronger and stronger. People often asked me if I believe in dieting. Yes; I believe in dieting on giants. Just de-vour, eat up every difficulty and trial that comes your way. You will wax stronger and stronger. A diet of

giants will keep you fresh and youthful. Just appropriate, masticate, digest, and assimilate one giant difficulty
after another. That diet, steadily persisted in, will
make *men,* nay *overcomers.*

Caleb wasn't afraid of "that which is high" like the
old man in Ecclesiastes 12:5, who lived on human
strength alone. No, he asked for a mountain:

> See the mountain tower high, frowning almost to
> the sky,
> And on its peak those cities fenced and great;
> Lo, the people cover in fear, for the Anakims live
> there,
> And each day with dread their coming they await.
> Oh, give me this mountain, for I am of the tribe
> of Praise,
> And, through the Victory of Israel, the Jubilee
> I'll raise.
> See the giants, how they flee! for our Lord, He
> fights for me,
> Lo, I drive them out for our Lord has said that I
> am able.

It is said concerning Billy Bray, the Cornish miner,
that at one time when he was praying, God promised
him a certain mountain and everyone upon it. At that
time there were three cottages on the mountainside.
He went into the first and led the people in it to the
Lord. Then he went into the second and there was a
miniature revival in that cottage as all its inhabitants
found Christ. Then he went into the third with like
results.

But that was not enough for Billy. He immediately
began to pray that the Lord would put some more
cottages on that mountain. Some time after this the
whole estate of which this mountain was a portion
was sold and a new village was erected. An Episcopal

church was built, but to Billy's great disgust the vicar of this church was a ritualist, an unsaved man. But Billy remembered God's promise to him and continued to beseech the throne. And William Haslam, the Episcopal rector in that church, was marvelously saved. Billy was delighted and went over to the vicar's home and caught up this very reverend gentleman and carried him around the house like a sack of potatoes, crying, "Parson's saved, parson's saved!"

There followed a gracious revival in that village in which Billy had his share. God gave him that mountain and every soul upon it.

But let us note especially two things about Caleb: First, he was of the tribe of Praise. Faith is the victory that overcometh, and praise is the voice of living faith. When the Israelites entered the promised land the Lord said, "Judah shall go up; behold, I have delivered the land into his hand" (Judges 1:2). Second, his name, Caleb means "dog." He says that God kept him alive because he *wholly* followed the Lord (Joshua 14:9). A dog asks no questions, has no suggestions to make. He simply follows his master whithersoever he goes.

The great Scotch philosopher Thomas Carlyle had a tiny Scotch terrier that was devoted to him. One night he sat by the fireside in his Highland cabin in the mountains, and a terrible storm raged without. Carlyle was suffering from one of the awful periods of depression to which he was liable and he felt so in tune with the shrieking tempest, rolling thunders, and flashing lightnings that he threw his plaid about him and went out into the storm bidding the tiny dog stay at home. But the faithful animal so besought him by whines and cries to be permitted to accompany him that he had not the heart to refuse, though he feared the little frail thing might perish on the mountain. As he walked along in the well-nigh impenetrable gloom he noticed the tiny speck of white fluff keeping close to his feet in every step. No peril could daunt, no darkness affright that living little heart. He had but one desire — to follow wholly.

If we will do that like Caleb, we too can ask for and obtain a mountain. Mountain dwellers see sunrise before those in the valleys; and the sun lingers longer with them at night. The air is clearer and purer there. The eagle gives one shriek when the clouds gather, and rises above them to the mountain.

"Flee as a bird to your mountain."

What mountain will you have?

Ararat: rest in a finished redemption for body, soul, and spirit.

Calvary: "Dying with Jesus, His death reckoned mine."

Carmel: where the fire falls from heaven and consumes the sacrifice.

Hermon: transfiguration. "Beholding as in a glass the glory of the Lord we are changed into His image."

Olivet: Behold He cometh!

8

His Face to the Wall

In Isaiah 38 we read that Hezekiah was "sick unto death," and that Isaiah the prophet came unto him and said: "Thus saith the Lord, Set thine house in order: for thou shalt die, and not live."

So the case was an absolutely hopeless one. Not only was the patient incurable by any remedies known to medical science, but God Himself had pronounced the death sentence upon him. "Thou shalt die and not live."

Yet, amazing fact Hezekiah did not die! He did not even set his house in order! What did he do? He turned his face to the wall. To *the wall;* away from man, even from Isaiah, the greatest of the prophets; away from his own sensations, symptoms, and sufferings; away from sympathizing friends and relatives; away from surgical skill (his case was a surgical one), to the wall.

What did he see there?

I read that when the famous English preacher Dr. Joseph Parker, when pastor of City Temple, London, crossed the ocean to minister in America, some young men who were most anxious to talk with him were sorely disappointed because he sat hour after hour gazing at the vast expanse of water as though unconscious of all else.

At last one of the group, more venturesome than the rest, said to him:

"What do you see there, Dr. Parker?"

"Nothing but God," he replied without turning his head.

Face to the wall! Blessed place where you see nothing but God! With face steadfastly turned to the wall, seeing nothing but God, with every faculty of his being concentrated on the beatific vision, there was imparted to Hezekiah the faith to which nothing is impossible (When God says "nothing" He means NOTHING), and the courage to go to God Himself, to pour out his heart before Him, and petition Him with tears for a prolongation of his life.

Because "all things are possible to him that believeth" (Mark 9:23), Isaiah received a command, before he had reached the middle court of the palace on his way out, to return to the king and announce the glad tidings that God had graciously acceded to his request and had added to his life fifteen years.

In all ages those who have done exploits for God have had to turn their faces resolutely to the wall, away from the human and everything connected therewith, to the divine.

Noah saved the human race from extinction by turning his face to the wall, where he found grace, and an ark, type of Christ, as the refuge of His people from judgment.

When everything human, Aaron included, failed Moses, and the people worshiped the golden calf, we read that he "returned to the Lord" who was ready to destroy the Israelitish nation if Moses, His chosen, had not stood before Him in the breach to turn away His wrath. But Moses had to turn his face to the wall.

David at Ziklag, when his possessions were in ashes, his loved ones taken into captivity, his followers, who had been so noted for their loyalty to him, ready to stone him, turned his face to the wall, and "encouraged himself in the Lord his God" (1 Samuel 30:6). The result was a great victory and much spoil.

Augustine, Bishop of Hippo, in the fifth century, tells us of a Carthage man of high rank, Innocentius by name, who was hopelessly ill of a malady for the cure of which he had endured a number of fearful operations without any improvement in his condition. At last the surgeons, while plainly stating that they feared it would cost his life, advised a final operative procedure as his only faint hope of surviving.

Augustine relates how the man with whom he had been asked to pray, "prostrated himself as if some one had forcibly thrust him down, and began to pray, with what earnestness, with what emotion, with what a flood of tears, with what agitation of his whole body, I might almost say with what suspension of his respiration by his groans and sobs, who shall attempt to describe? . . . For my part I could not pray. This alone, inwardly and briefly, I said: "Lord what prayers of Thy children wilt Thou ever grant if Thou grant not these?' For nothing seemed more probable than that he should die praying."

He goes on to tell us that when the surgeons came and removed the dressings they found the diseased tissues perfectly healed and normal in every respect. Innocentius, in short, turned to the wall and found there a God for whom nothing is too hard.

Martin Luther knew what it was to turn his face to the wall in utter despair of all human aid. When he found Philip Melancthon, his God-given helper in the Protestant Reformation, in the very act and article of death, eyes set, speech gone, consciousness almost gone, face fallen, Luther turned away from the awful scene to the window, and there called on God, urging upon Him all the promises he could repeat from the Scriptures, and adding, with incredible boldness that God must hear and answer now if He would ever have the petitioner trust Him again.

Melancthon, writing to a friend, said, "I should have been a dead man had I not been recalled from death itself by the coming of Luther." Luther wrote as follows to friends: "Philip is very well. . . . I found him dead but by an evident miracle of God he lives."

I am associated in the Lord's work with a dear sister who had seven major operations performed on her by some of the best surgeons in this or any other country. Her friends jokingly say that everything was removed except her brains. I can testify that they are intact and fertile of many splendid expedients for advancing the kingdom of our Lord and Saviour Jesus Christ.

After all this surgery adhesive inflammation set in, and she was simply "glued together inside," to quote her own words. Every effort was made to relieve this condition but all in vain. Lying on her hospital cot dying, she, like Hezekiah, turned her face to the wall. There she saw Jesus only. Such childlike confidence and unclouded trust came with the sight that she knew the work was done. She was prayed with for healing and saw herself submerged in depths of burning white light. "In Him was life and the life was the light of men." From the day, nine years ago, she has done two days' work every day of her life. I am a constant witness of her unceasing activity.

I had thirty-five blessed years added to my life because I dared, when dying from the abuse of narcotics, to turn my face to the wall and cast myself upon God. I said to myself as I drew a sigh of utmost relief, "It can't fail now because it's ALL GOD." It didn't fail, and I don't know how many more blessed years He is going to grant me, if the Lord should tarry.

I feel it to be a priceless privilege to live at this period of history when we have golden opportunities of turning our faces to the wall and taking victory over all the power of hell through faith in our all-conquering Christ.

We are co-workers together with God, and our work is to *believe* on Him whom God hath sent. If we don't believe, we are not workers but ciphers, and worse. God has made man's cooperation necessary in the plan of redemption. *"If thou canst believe, all things are possible to him that believeth."*

The Lord Jesus awaits the trembling, tearful cry of the father of the demon-possessed boy, "Lord, I believe; help thou my unbelief," before He speaks the word of power: "I charge thee, come out of him, and enter no more into him."

The eyes of the Lord are running to and fro throughout the whole earth to show Himself strong in the behalf of them whose heart is perfect toward Him, that is, those who fully trust Him.

I am sure God is *sufficient* for "these things," the things that he allows to come into your life and mine, the tests spiritual, mental, physical, financial. If we will but turn our faces to the wall and see nothing but God, we shall find ourselves more than conquerors in all of them.

Nay, more. I believe that God will use us, if we will look away from all else to Him alone, to mitigate the awful conditions that surround us, to heal the broken-hearted, to proclaim liberty to the captives, and the opening of the prison to them that are bound. But He has made man's *faith* a determining factor in the execution of the divine purposes; and the indispensable prerequisite to being so used is that we turn our faces to the wall and see nothing but God.

9

A Song of Resurrection

"He brought me up . . . out of an horrible pit, out of the miry clay, and set my feet upon a rock, and established my goings. *And he hath put a new song in my mouth*" (Psalm 40:2, 3).

Here we find a man crying to God out of "an horrible pit." A pit of horrors, indeed, for the original implies a place of "chaos, confusion, conflict, noise, tumult, dimness, darkness, disorder, despair, death, and destruction." Rotherham translates it "the destroying pit," so all in it are doomed by the mere fact that they are there.

How did this man, who is typical of every man who has ever lived from Adam down, get there? Did God, who made him, put him there? Never. "The Lord God planted a garden eastward in Eden; and there he put the man whom he had formed. And out of the ground made the Lord God to grow every tree that is pleasant to the sight, and good for food" (Genesis 2:8, 9).

I have gazed enraptured at gardens made by human hands, which were so beautiful that they took my breath away, but what must have been the exquisite loveliness of this garden planted by the divine hand that put the shine into the stars, the majesty into the mountains, the sacred beauty into the dawn, the glory into the sunset, and tinted the petal of the rose!

Man had only to dwell there amidst noble trees, emerald green turf, gorgeous blossoms, flashing fountains, singing birds, beautiful, sleek animals, who fawned on him as their God-given head, and enjoy uninterrupted communion and fellowship with the Author of all this beauty, the Creator of the universe, and the Bestower of every good and perfect gift.

Whence, then, the pit? It was Satan, that malign and mysterious being, once the "anointed cherub . . . upon the holy mountain of God" in the mineral Eden of Ezekiel 28, with every precious stone for his covering, whose heart was lifted up because of his beauty, and who corrupted his wisdom by reason of his brightness, who dug the pit of sin — rebellion against divine authority — and lured our first parents into his trap.

The bait was the knowledge of good and evil. The prize was won, but at what a cost! For Adam and Eve fell into the pit; and all their progeny, from that day to this, were born there. And from the pit there is no human way of escape.

Men have sought out many inventions, embellished their pit dwellings with magnificent works of art, perfected systems of philosophy, even erected retaining walls, and laid down paving stones of ethical culture to prevent people from sinking deeper in the mire, but no man has ever been able to find a way out. In other words, with all the genius manifested by pit dwellers, there is no power in the pit to extricate anyone from its depths.

And when all is said and done, in spite of scientific

discoveries, rapid transportation on earth and sea and in the sky, radio, and other wonders, the pit is the pit still, and it is a horrible pit; the Bible says so. Some are deeper in the mire than others, but all alike have sinned, and the wages of sin is death.

As there is no power in the pit to deliver, it is evident that if anyone is to escape eternal doom, aid must come from above, and that is precisely what happened. One day, while heaven resounded with anthems of praise, Jesus Christ, the effulgence of the Father's glory and the expression of His substance, rose — "and the light in heaven grew dimmer as He left His father's side" — and came, down, *down*, DOWN, from the rainbow circled throne on the sapphire pavement, down from the adoration of the living creatures who cease not day nor night crying, "Holy, Holy, Holy!" Down from the glory which He had with the Father before all worlds. Down past whirling planets, burning suns, and rotating systems, to this dark world, to the very verge of the noisome pit crying: "Lo, I come: in the volume of the book it is written of me . . . to do thy will, O my God" (Psalm 40:7, 8).

Plunged into the deepest depths of that awful abyss of darkness, a voice was heard from heaven proclaiming: "Deliver . . . from going down to the pit: I have found a ransom" (Job 33:24).

"But none of the ransomed ever knew how deep was the water crossed; nor how dark was the night that the Lord passed through e'er He found His sheep that was lost. Away in the desert He heard its cry, sick and helpless and ready to die."

For He went down to the very "roots of the mountains," below your sins and mine, and from the awful profundities ascended a cry to the Father: "Thou wilt not leave my soul in hell, neither wilt thou suffer thine Holy One to see corruption" (Acts 2:27).

And God inclined unto Him and heard His cry and brought Him up, and set His feet upon a rock, and established His goings, and put a new song into His mouth, a Song of Resurrection. And, thank God, He did not come up alone but brought with Him, out of the pit, all who through all the ages should believe on Him.

By faith we make His death ours. By faith we make His resurrection ours — ours the security, stability, safety, strength, and steadfastness of the rock, for "I hold not the Rock but the Rock holds me." Ours the Song on the Rock, the Song of Resurrection.

Oh! There's a song I fain would sing,
   A song of praise to my Saviour King;
It is high as the height where He intercedes,
   It is sweet as the tone in which He pleads,
It is low as the reach of His mighty arm,
   It is strong as His power over sin and harm;
To sing this song have you been set free?
   He can sing it through you,
He can sing it through me.

This song of praise shall yet be sung,
   In every tribe, by every tongue;
The angels desire its notes to swell,
   But redemptive love they cannot tell.
Creation groaneth this song to hear,
   All shackles melt as it strikes the ear;
Then the sons of God this world will see.
   Shall He sing it through you?
Shall He sing it through me?

Many years ago, in New York City, they brought a poor degraded girl into an institution. The love of Christ in a Christian sister had won her from the life of the streets. I said to myself, "A familiar type enough!"

But was she such a familiar type after all? Poor, despised, desolate, and alone, with ragged garments and shoes out of which the water was squeezing at each step. That was familiar enough; only too familiar. But there was a light in her eye, a purpose in her bearing, and above all a song continually on her lips that caught and riveted my attention in spite of myself, cultured heathen that I was at that time.

She seemed to have everything of the hardest — the business end of the broom and scrubbing brush. But the sweeping and scrubbing were just an obligato to the solo that she sang continually:

> "On Christ, the solid Rock I stand,
> All other ground is sinking sand."

Christ had raised her from the death of sin, and she was singing the Song of Resurrection.

"Sarah," I inquired, "Why do you sing all the time?"

"Because I'm happy."

"I suppose you think you're saved?" (I had seen cases before and thought I recognized the symptoms.)

"No, Ma'am."

"You don't think you're saved?" I inquired, filled with wonderment.

"No, Ma'am; *I know it.*" And off she went with her scrub pail, singing, "On Christ the Solid Rock I stand."

Well might she sing. She was on the Rock and she knew it. On the Rock she was delivered from everything that belongs to the pit — the guilt, condemnation, power, and penalty of sin, and its outworkings in the body . . . *sickness and debility.* Praise God!

If the pit is not the rock, neither is the rock the pit.

Satan will try to pursue you with phantoms of darkness, sin, and sickness, but refuse them in the power of His resurrection.

Where are *you?* There are but two places for mortals. The horrible pit, and the Rock of Ages. If you are in the horrible pit, cry unto God and He will deliver you, for "whosoever shall call upon the name of the Lord shall be saved" (Romans 10:13). If you are on the Rock, sing the new song that God has put in your mouth, the "Song of Resurrection."

10

Spring Medicine

It is about the time of the year that Grandmother used to give the children all around a dose of what she called "spring medicine."

"What is it good for, Grandmother?"

"Good for everything. Cleanses your whole system; strengthens you; increases your resistance to disease; prevents sickness getting hold of you. It's a tonic that vitalizes you and makes it a joy to live and work and play."

"What is in it, Grandmother?"

"Everything good: sulphur, cleansing and purging; camomile, clearing your blood and skin; sassafras to stir up your system; a little salts and senna, burdock, dandelion, and other herbs, and good old black New Orleans molasses."

Dear old Grandmother's "spring medicine!" How bitter it was and yet how sweet! "Bittersweet" we called it.

That is just like our "spring medicine."

You remember the little book that the angel gave to John, the Beloved, when for the Word of God and the testimony of Jesus Christ, he was in exile on that lonely rock, six miles by twelve miles, in the Aegean Sea, called the Isle of Patmos; where when every earthly door was closed, he saw one opened in heaven. The angel told him to take the book and eat it up, and it should be in his mouth sweet as honey, though it would make his belly bitter.

God believes in bitters, and prescribes them when we need them. When Esther was being prepared to go in to the king she was six months in sweet odors, and six months with oil of myrrh. Bitter, bitter myrrh! And they tell us, ancient cosmeticians — oh yes, they had beauty parlors then too — that it was the oil of myrrh that had the marvelous property of removing every blemish from the skin and making it like living alabaster.

So don't let us be afraid of the bitter in the prescription, but take God's Spring Medicine, for we need it in the spring, and in the summer, autumn and winter as well. Grandmother's "spring medicine" may have been one huge blunder, or big mistake, like some other prescriptions, but there is no mistake about God's remedies. They are unfailing, and we surely need them.

Let us pick up the crystal vial and drink from Psalm 103:1-5: "Bless the Lord, O my soul: and all that is within me, bless his holy Name."

Now notice the label on the bottle, the instructions for taking the medicine (v. 2): "Forget not *all* His benefits." Don't leave out any part of the medicine.

It reminds you of a loving mother packing her boy's trunk, putting everything he can possibly need into it, on the eve of his departure for college, and then writing a note and placing it on the very top of all, where it must catch his eye, saying:

"My darling son: Don't forget that your heavy

underwear is at the bottom of the trunk in case the weather should turn cold. Be sure to wear it if you need it. And your best suit is on top. Put it on if you are invited out. Don't forget your good ties in a box and your socks to match in another box. Mother loves you and wants you to be well and happy every moment. If you put your hand away down in the right-hand corner near the front you will find a big jar of those nut cookies you are so fond of, and beside it a little tin box of Mother's chocolate fudge."

God has packed everything we need into this treasure casket we call the Bible, and He loves us so much that He even condescends to remind us of "His benefits" — all of them.

"Benefits" are available to members of lodges bestowing them — at least so I am informed — who have their dues all paid up and are in good standing. Thank God those conditions need not affright us for, as the old hymn says,

Jesus paid it all.
    All to Him I owe,
Sin had left a crimson stain,
    He washed it white as snow.

And as to our standing, He took our place and gave us His. He hung on the cross, where we belonged, and made us to be "accepted in the Beloved." So let us drink freely of the medicine He has provided for us. "Who forgiveth all thine iniquities" (v. 3). Yes, it's there.

"Who healeth all our diseases." Praise God for that! Don't forget that great and glorious "benefit." Claim it, receive it, rejoice in it.

But you are only half healed when you do that.

There remains still in our mortal bodies the tendency to depreciation, disintegration, destruction. You might be well today and break all your bones tomorrow, or suffer some awful injury, or have a stroke of paralysis, if it were not for the keeping power of God. So quickly gulp down the next dose provided. "Forget not *all* His benefits."

"Who redeemeth thy life from destruction" (v. 4). You are walking through death all the time. As David said, "There is but a step between me and death" (1 Samuel 20:3). But God redeemed David's life from destruction, and He has promised to redeem yours.

And here is another dose, and oh, it is so sweet! "Who crowneth thee with loving kindness and tender mercies" (v. 4). It seems to me that people who have never experienced the healing power of Jesus in their own bodies cannot fully appreciate Him.

But the very best part of this wonderful medicine is yet to come. Tilt the crystal vial up and don't lose a single drop. "Forget not *all* His benefits."

"Who satisfieth thy mouth with good things so that thy youth is renewed like the eagle's" (v. 5).

That is divine life after divine healing. How few people will drain the crystal vial!

But you need it all. You need continuous healing when you are well, as well as when you are sick. You need to be lifted above the plane where Satan can inoculate you with his germs. You need the overflowing life of God in your body as well as in your soul and spirit. God is holding the precious elixir of life to your lips this moment. "Drink, yea drink abundantly, Beloved," He cries to you and me.

11

He Giveth His Beloved Sleep

There is nothing more essential to our well-being — physical, mental, and perhaps even spiritual — than an adequate amount of refreshing, natural sleep.

Gene Tunney once stated in the course of an interview that, in his opinion, plenty of healthy sleep is of more importance than anything else in the training of an athlete. He rated it as of higher value than proper diet, suitable exercise, "work outs," or any other part of the training.

"If he sleep he shall do well," but how to make him sleep is sometimes a problem. It has proved insoluble by medical authorities until the present hour.

God, and God alone, can give sleep. You may place yourself in the most favorable surroundings, pillow your head on down, let the balmy breezes play gently over your couch, secure stillness, and count whole flocks of sheep, but unless the finger of Omnipotence touches your closed eyelids and distills through your frame that blessed blissful, delicious something which we call "sleep" there is no slumber for you. Not even a king can command it: "On that night could not the king (Ahasuerus) sleep" (Esther 6:1).

In speaking on this subject I am on familiar ground, for I suffered from insomnia for years and could only lose consciousness by putting myself under the influence of the most powerful narcotics, regular "knockout drops," and I can testify that during that time *I never slept.*

Though I used to turn as purple as grapes, and make such awful strangling sounds with respiration that my friends many times never expected me to awaken again, I *never slept* till God, for Christ's sake, delivered me from that awful incubus of morphine addiction that was crushing me. Then God gave me sleep, and *I slept.*

The difference between that blessed natural slumber from the hand of God, that heavenly dew gently distilling on my closed eyelids, and the awful torture of the condition brought about by brain-twisting drugs, was as great as that between heaven and hell.

Does someone ask, "How am I to get this refreshing sleep from God?" Notice the words of Scripture: "He *giveth* his beloved sleep." It is a gift and you have only to receive it.

John reposed on Jesus' breast. There is room there for you and me too. He was called "Beloved" because he took the place. You can take it, too.

Dr. A. B. Simpson says somewhere in his God-given writings, "You have not gone far if you cannot lay your head on Jesus' breast and sleep by faith." What are the essentials for this?

First, a clear conscience made pure by the precious blood of Jesus.

We read in Acts 12 of the apostle Peter, doomed to execution by Herod, guarded by sixteen Roman soldiers, bound with chains, keepers before the door of his dungeon, sweetly sleeping! What a fulfillment of the promise, "When thou liest down, thou shalt not be afraid: . . . thy sleep shall be sweet" (Proverbs 3:24). Sleep has healed more sickness, relieved more pain, removed more symptoms than any medicine known to man.

Take up your Bible and read how God put Adam (Genesis 2:21), Abraham (Genesis 15:12), and Jacob to sleep, though the latter had only stones for his pillow. The hardness of his couch did not prevent his having dreams of heaven and angel visitants.

"But, doctor, are you correct in saying that there are no drugs that will induce sleep? I thought that there were many that would put one to sleep: hypnotics, narcotics, sedatives, etc. Do you mean to say that there are no agents that will produce sleep?"

Emphatically yes. I mean to say just that. It is true that there are drugs that will produce drowsiness, torpor, partial or complete unconsciousness for shorter or longer periods — they will sometimes make you sleep the sleep of death — but these are for the most part virulent poisons, many of them habit-forming, and not one of them can impart natural sleep.

> Peace, perfect Peace,
> In this dark world of sin,
> The Blood of Jesus
> Whispers "Peace" within.

If you cannot sleep ask God if all is well with your soul. "Though your sins be as scarlet they shall be made as white as snow." Then simply take sweet sleep just as you take salvation. Praise God for it before you feel it, and before you know it you will be fast asleep.

There are times when God wants to talk to us as He did to little Samuel. A sister told me that one night she could not sleep so she asked God why this was, and He answered her that He wanted to talk to her for a while. So she listened to the whispers of Jesus and when the message was finished praised Him for it. Then He said very tenderly: "Now go to sleep my child," and she slept. "He giveth His beloved sleep."

12

"As They Went"

"And as he entered into a certain village, there met him ten men that were lepers, which stood afar off: And they lifted up their voices, and said, Jesus, Master, have mercy on us. And when he saw them, he said unto them, Go show yourselves unto the priests. And it came to pass, that, as they went, they were cleansed. And one of them, when he saw that he was healed, turned back, and with a loud voice glorified God, and fell down on his face at his feet, giving him thanks: and he was a Samaritan. And Jesus answering said, Were there not ten cleansed? but where are the nine? There are not found that returned to give glory to God, save this stranger. And he said unto him, Arise, go thy way: thy faith hath made thee whole" (Luke 17:12-19).

The healing of the ten lepers is worthy of especially careful study, presenting as it does features not found in connection with other miracles of healing performed by our Lord Jesus Christ during His earthly ministry.

First, it is a *group* healing. We have here ten men, a number that is often associated in the Scriptures with tests, or trials. For instance, for ten days the children of Judah at the court of Babylon, including Daniel, were tested, or tried, on a diet of pulse, after which they were found ten times better than all the magicians and astrologers in the realm, and fairer and fatter in flesh than all the children which did eat the king's meat. Likewise, the church at Smyrna was promised ten days of tribulation to try them so that the faithful unto death might be awarded a crown of life.

In the case of the healing of the ten lepers it would seem to be God's remedy for disease, His Word ("He sent his word, and healed them," Psalm 107:20) which is tested or tried.

In establishing the therapeutic value of any remedy in a certain disease it is quite usual to try it out on a group of sufferers from that particular malady, and that is precisely what was done in the case of the ten lepers. These men differed no doubt in other respects, mentally, morally, and socially, but they had one thing in common, their hopeless misery, for they were — all ten of them — lepers.

Even in their leprosy they differed no doubt, for among ten cases some would necessarily be more aggravated than others. There would be those still in the incipience of the disease, others further advanced with more marked symptoms, and others still presenting the appalling changes, such as sloughing of large portions of the flesh producing hideous deformity, which characterize the last stages, in which almost all resemblance to humanity is sometimes obliterated.

Lepers usually hid themselves from the public gaze in their lairs, for they were not permitted to mingle with their kind for fear of contagion. How then can we account for this public gathering of sufferers from the loathsome disease? Whence did they derive the courage to take such a daring step?

Some way there had been borne to them by the "wind that bloweth where it listeth" a Name, a mighty Name, a Name above every name, Jesus of Nazareth, who healed even the leper, and faith came by hearing, and they determined to reach Him if they had to imperil their lives to accomplish it. Hence this pitiful assemblage.

Rabbis, doctors of the Law, scribes, and Pharisees, would have recoiled from them as from poisonous reptiles. Priests and Levites would have drawn their robes tight about them to avoid pollution. But Jesus, the spotless Lamb of God, invites sinners, and sick folks, no matter how awful their depravity, or loathsome their disease, to come to Him and find rest.

And when He saw them, standing afar off, as the Law bade them (Thank God we under grace are brought nigh by the blood of Christ), but lifting up their voices determinedly, concertedly, in the piteous chorus, "Jesus, Master, have mercy on us!" He replied immediately. He always does. There is not a soul in existence who dare assert that Jesus ever failed to answer when he cried to Him for mercy. He "saw" them through and through and recognized that it was a *heart* cry, and He answered it.

But what an answer? How startling His reply! How unexpected His command! "Go show yourselves unto the priests." "Go *show!*" Why, they had been industriously hiding themselves, concealing, covering, cloaking, for they well knew that they were vile beyond expression, rotten, putrid, decaying, dying on their feet.

"Go show yourselves *unto the priests?*" The officials

charged with the responsibility of making the minutest inspection, and declaring the leper an outcast from human society, if symptoms of the dread disease were discovered, also were empowered to issue a clean bill of health to the cleansed leper which restored him to his privileges as one of God's people.

The word Jesus spoke to them healed, and commanded them, because they were healed, to present themselves to the priests for official certification of the fact. Please note that they, not one, two or three, four, five or six of them, but all ten, went. And as *they went,* not as they talked about it, sang about it, or even shouted about it, but *as they did it,* they were, all ten of them, the man in the last stages quite as much as the one who had but recently become infected with the deadly virus, cleansed, and had something to show that they were not afraid or ashamed to display before a whole conference of ecclesiastics, namely, perfect soundness through faith in the name of Jesus of Nazareth.

I am altogether devoid of theatrical aspirations, but I am free to confess that ever since the Lord healed me of hopeless conditions, resulting from morphine addiction, I have been in the "show business" (it is thirty-five years now), and never expect to retire. I long to tell with every breath what the Lord Jesus Christ is ready to do for the most hopeless cases of sin and sickness, and to point to myself as a monument of saving grace, to "Go and show."

This Scripture verse was once brought home to me with great force during a time of fierce testing. I was working in a government office, and also holding a number of meetings a week, and my eyes failed under the continuous strain. I felt sure that I could secure a prolonged leave of absence with salary, six months or even longer, by making application in the proper quarter, but I prayed earnestly before doing so.

To my surprise the healing of the ten lepers was brought vividly to my consciousness, and on reading the passage the words *"as they went"* stood out from the page as though they were for me personally. So certain was I of this that I abandoned all idea of applying for leave and was almost instantaneously relieved of all trouble in using my eyes. But it happened *"as I went."* I had to do some "wenting" before deliverance was manifested.

Do not fail to note that ten went and ten were cleansed. God's remedy for all disease met the test as it always does. No matter what the ailment, whether incipient or advanced, how young or old the sufferer, Jesus never fails.

Leprosy is a type of sin, and there is no remedy for it but a cry of Jesus. Have you called upon the name of the Lord? If not, come in your sin and sickness, call upon Him, step out on His Word in the direction which He indicates and you will have something to show, for you can say, "Behold the Lamb of God, which taketh away the sin of the world" (John 1:29).

But now comes a sharper test. Ten were leprous; ten called on the name of the Lord; ten were cleansed. But only one, and he a stranger of whom nothing was expected, returned to give thanks; only one cast himself at the feet of Jesus; only one glorified God, and he was a Samaritan.

"And Jesus answering said, Were there not ten cleansed? but where are the nine?"

During the last thirty-five years I have known

directly and indirectly of the healing of thousands by the power of God through the grace of the Lord Jesus Christ. Where are they today?

If they were all like the Samaritan, at the feet of Jesus, I believe that many of the problems that constantly confront us in Christian work would be solved.

Shall we not like David who, when men went in jeopardy of their lives to fetch him water from the well of Bethlehem, refused to drink it but poured it out unto the Lord, say of our lives, redeemed from destruction by His death:

> "Love so amazing, so divine,
> Shall have my life,
> My love, my all."

13

Thrust Out from the Land

"And it came to pass, that, as the people pressed upon him to hear the word of God, he stood by the lake of Gennesaret, and saw two ships standing by the lake: but the fishermen were gone out of them, and were washing their nets. And He entered into one of the ships, which was Simon's, and prayed him that he would thrust out a little from the land. And he sat down, and taught the people out of the ship. Now when he had left speaking, he said unto Simon, Launch out into the deep, and let down your nets for a draught. And Simon answering said unto him, Master, we have toiled all the night, and have taken nothing: nevertheless at thy word I will let down the net. And when they had this done, they inclosed a great multitude of fishes: and their net brake . . . And Jesus said unto Simon, Fear not; from henceforth thou shalt catch men" (Luke 5:1-6, 10).

Behold this picture painted by the master Artist, the Holy Spirit! The scene is laid beside the lake of Gennesaret, the time is the early morning and the rays of the sun are making "Blue Galilee" glint like a pavement of sapphire. On its shores is a press of eager men, women, and children. Hungry? Yes; but for more than the bread that perisheth. Thirsty? Famishing, with a thirst that no earthly fountain can slake.

There, beside that sea, stands One who is Himself the living Bread that came down from heaven, the Dispenser of the water of life of which when any drink they thirst no more. Mystery of mysteries! He *stands*, inactive, while masses of people press upon Him, not only that their sicknesses may be healed, and their empty stomachs filled with loaves and fishes, but that they may hear the Word.

Theirs is a profound hunger, an all-consuming thirst. "Man doth not live by bread only, but by every word that proceedeth out of the mouth of the Lord doth man live" (Deuteronomy 8:3). They are dimly, dumbly conscious of their need of life. Like Bunyan's pilgrim who ran from the city of Destruction crying:

> "Life! life! eternal life!
> 'Tis life of which our nerves are scant,
> 'Tis life, not death, for which we pant."

And yet Jesus, who came that we might have life, stands apparently unmoved. He is not even looking at the starving, struggling mass of humanity that presses upon Him. Why? Because God is not only going to do exactly what He says, but He is going to do it exactly *as* He says. He has tied Himself irrevocably to human cooperation in the work of redemption. He has made man's faith a determining factor in the execution of divine purposes.

"We . . . as workers together with him (Gr. fellow workmen), beseech you also that ye receive not the grace of God in vain" (2 Corinthians 6:1). He who has constituted us His fellow workmen is He who hath said, "My counsel shall stand, and I will do all my pleasure . . . I have spoken it, I will also bring it to pass; I have purposed it, I will also do it."

God cannot fail, so man's cooperation in the work of redemption cannot fail. Individuals may fail; let us be passionately determined that, by God's grace, we shall not be among the number. But God's purposes will still be carried out according to His plan, in every detail, if He has to raise up from the stones under our feet "children to Abraham," in other words, stagger-nots who will, like Paul, believe God, that it shall be *even as it was told them.*

What is the Lord Jesus looking at? Study the picture limned by the brush of divine inspiration. He is gazing at two poor little ships standing idle on the shore, and a small group of bedraggled, discouraged fishermen, who have abondoned them, and are washing their nets preparatory to hanging them up to dry.

> I have toiled all night and for many a day,
>   They say there are fish in the sea,
> But I've caught nothing, my labor is vain;
>   There cometh no increase to me.
> I will wash out my net and hang it away,
>   And my fishing boat draw to the shore;
> They are useless to me; I will cast out my net
>   In these barren sea waters no more.

Did you ever feel like that? Did you ever look like that? Do you feel like that now? If so it shows in your face and you look like it.

I was rather dismayed on one occasion by something that happened. I was walking up a very steep hill from the ocean when a lady and gentleman in a car stopped and asked me if they might give me a lift.

(I was laden with parcels.) They were strangers to me but I got into the car most thankfully. We exchanged a sentence or two — I don't remember just what I said — but the gentleman replied, "You must be a Christian." I felt like saying, "Don't I look like one?" For I felt they should have known it the minute they saw me. Evidently I didn't have on what a well-dressed Christian should wear, the outshining of the inner glory. Let your light shine; don't pull the blinds down.

Well, even if we are conscious that we have not been feeling and looking just as we ought, perhaps we don't look any worse than Peter and James and John did that day, yet Jesus headed straight for their ships and took possession. Let us give Him a royal welcome, for I am sure He is coming to each of us this very hour!

And as He enters He gives the word of command which must be uttered, *and obeyed*, before those poor hungry souls on the shore can get so much as a crumb, for we are working together with God and cannot be dispensed with. Listen to the words: "He entered into one of the ships, which was Simon's and *prayed* him that he would thrust out a *little* from the land."

The Lord Jesus Christ, "the God-Man, who threw the stars in their orbits and spheres into space; who swung the earth a trinket at His wrist; whom the winds and waves obeyed, pleading pitifully with His creatures to thrust out a little from land. Oh, believe Me a little at least. Thrust out from land. Don't hug the shore so tight. Oh, thrust out from the shore of sensation, sight, sound, feelings, symptoms, human experiences, intellectual deductions. Thrust out from it all."

Oh, it's heaven below to thrust out from land! Then Jesus can teach from your ship and the poor starving folks on the shore get something to eat. Thrust out! How far? Just as far as you like. You can have just as much of the supernatural, the miraculous, the divine as you will take. The "age of miracles" is *now* for the one who will dare to thrust out.

After "Thrust out" comes the command, "Launch out." We may just as well do it. We are confronted with the supernatural these days. Hell is moved from beneath and it takes the divine to cope with it. As we launch out, heaven comes to the rescue. The stars in their courses fight for us. Faith achieves the impossible and a draught of fishes is caught after a fruitless night of weary toil.

14

Singing Sickness Away

I speak from personal experience of the healing power that flows from some of our hymns. And why should I not do so? "He sent his word, and healed them" (Psalm 107:20), and they are simply the Word of God in a musical setting.

When at the last gasp from mortal illness which, but for God's miraculous intervention, would have terminated my life many years ago, I went to a meeting in church located four blocks from the place where I lay dying, walking every step of the way, and it was raining.

Like Paul, I can solemnly say, "I went up by revelation," and I should never have arrived at my destination if this had not been the case. An impossibility was achieved through me, *not by me,* but by God "who quickeneth the dead."

When I reached the church I sat on the cushions on a seat near the entrance, and was not particularly alive to my surroundings until the strains of an old, a very old hymn which has been called the crowning hymn of Methodism, "Jesus, Lover of my Soul," floated to my consciousness.

An old preacher said, "A song may reach us where a sermon flies," and the healing message of that old hymn flowed over my sinking soul and shattered body like "ointment poured forth."

> *All* my trust on Thee is stayed;
>   All my help from *Thee* I bring . . .
> Thou, O Christ art *all* I want;
>   More than *all* in Thee I find;
> Raise the fallen, cheer the faint,
>   *Heal the sick*, and lead the blind . . .
>
> Plenteous grace with Thee is found,
>   Grace to cover all my sin;
> *Let the healing streams abound.*
>   Make and keep me pure within.
>
> Thou of life the fountain art,
>   Freely let me take of Thee;
> Spring Thou up within my heart,
>   Rise to all eternity.

My recovery dated from that hour, and the experience led me to search hymns, ancient and modern, for more of the blessed elixir of life. Here I wish to share with others the rich treasures I unearthed.

We find divine healing in the "Song of Moses," which the children of Israel were commanded to sing and to teach to their children, as it should "not be forgotten out of the mouths of their seed" (Deuteronomy 31:21). How inspiring to their faith to join in with a mighty chorus singing the majestic words, "I, even I, am he, and there is no god with me: I kill, and I *make alive;* I wound, and I *heal*" (Deuteronomy 32:39).

The Holy Spirit-inspired Praise Book, the Psalms,

is filled with the precious truth that God provides for our physical as well as our spiritual well-being.

As the Psalms have been used in public worship all down the centuries, and are still so used throughout Christendom, including the Roman and Greek churches, it follows that even in ages of darkness and apostasy men have *sung* healing through trust in Christ, though they have not always had the faith and courage to preach and practice it.

Psalm 107 is largely used in public worship; the refrain, "Oh that men would praise the Lord for his goodness, and for his wonderful works to the children of men!" being sometimes sung by thousands of voices.

How clearly the relationship between sin and sickness and the unfailing remedy to be found in God alone is brought out in verses 17-20. I quote from Dr. Alexander Maclaren's version, *The Expositor's Bible*, Volume III:

"Foolish men, because of their transgression, and because of their iniquities, brought on themselves affliction. All feel their soul loathed, and they drew near to the gates of death. And they cried to Jehovah in their distress. From their troubles He saved them. He sent His Word and healed them, and rescued them from their graves."

From a hymn by Ambrose, Bishop of Milan (340-397 A. D.), it would seem that the dauntless old saint who rebuked the emperor, Theodosius the Great, and refused to permit him to enter the church until he publicly confessed his terrible sin in massacring some of the inhabitants of Thessalonia, also withstood Satan's power in his own body and claimed a death like that of Moses, whose eye was not dimmed, nor his natural force abated, when he was lifted out of mortality by the kiss of Divinity. Here is the verse in question:

> Grant to life's day a calm unclouded ending;
>   An eye *untouched by shadows of decay;*
> The brightness of a holy deathbed blending
>   With dawning glories of eternal day.

Thank God that modern hymns on healing abound! We cannot have too many of them, providing they are inspired by the Holy Spirit, for in that case they are, like Paul's gospel, *"according to the Scriptures."* Praise God for appointing singers to go before us in this conflict!

But let us never forget that it is not enough to listen appreciatively to these songs of victory over Satan's power to attack our bodies; not even enough to join in the chorus, no matter how lustily. We must not only confess with our mouths the Lord Jesus, but *we must believe in our hearts that God hath raised Him from the dead,* which means that we, as we abide in Him, are lifted clean off the plane where sickness can have dominion over us.

"The law of the Spirit of life in Christ Jesus hath made me free from the law of sin and death" (Romans 8:2). Disease is the death process, death working in our physical beings. Thank God for healing in hymnology! Thank God that we can "sing sickness away" if we will only believe unreservedly on the One who bore it away in His own body on the cross of Calvary! Thank God that "Christ is All!"

Let me give one instance of this from my personal experience. A certain sister found herself in the midst of a physical ordeal that ordinarily would have meant the attendance of physicians, nurses, etc., and medical, and possibly surgical, measures of a grave nature. But, led of God, she appointed singers ("praisers," Hebrew), and herself led the choir in the chorus of the familiar hymn:

> Christ is all, all in all,
> Christ is all in all.
> Christ is all, all in all,
> Yes, *Christ is all in all!*

They sang and sang and *sang!* And still they sang till God did what no human power could have accomplished, and heaven came down their souls to meet as "Glory crowned the mercy seat."